BRUISED but Beautiful

BRUISED

but

Beautiful

Comforting Words for your Grieving Heart

TRUDY M. JOHNSON

BRUISED BUT BEAUTIFUL

Copyright © 2025 by Trudy M. Johnson

Written by Trudy M. Johnson

Published by: U Are Not Alone Foundation – Trudy M. Johnson
Printed in United States of America
June 2025

ISBN: **979-8-218-70410-0**

Disclaimer:
This book is based on true events. Some names and identifying details have been changed to protect the privacy of individuals involved.

Printed in United States of America

TABLE OF CONTENTS

DEDICATION

To every heart that has faced the unthinkable — the loss of a child or someone deeply loved. To those who wake up each day carrying the weight of absence, feeling the ache of empty spaces. May these words offer you a place to rest, and that even in the depths of grief, there is still beauty waiting to be discovered within.

This book is for **you**.
For your strength, your courage, and the love that endures beyond the pain.

— With all my heart,
Trudy M. Johnson

PURPOSE

This book was born from brokenness, but it is not a book about defeat. It is a book about becoming.

Bruised but beautiful is my offering to those who have loved deeply, lost painfully, and are learning to live again with grace. I wrote these pages through tears, in silence, in prayer, and in sacred stillness- because I know what it feels like to ache with grief and still hope for healing.

Each page is filled with heartfelt quotes, poems, prayers, scriptures, and meditations. My purpose in writing this is simple; to wrap arms of comfort around your weary heart, reminding you that you are not alone. Others have walked this path, feeling the same ache, asking the same questions, and searching for light in the darkness. This book offers comfort and connection, showing you that even when life leaves you bruised, you can still be beautiful — because bruises may fade, but the beauty that emerges from your pain can last forever. That is the heart of *Bruised But Beautiful.*

BRUISED but Beautiful

QUOTES

"I am bruised but beautiful because I've walked through the fire of loss and came out holding the flame of my child's love."

There's a unique pain in losing someone so close to you - a pain that bruises the soul in ways that words can't fully capture. It feels like walking through fire, with grief burning away every certainty you once held. But even in the flames, not everyone is destroyed. What remains is the indestructible bond of love –a flame that lights the darkest moments and soothes the bruises of the soul.

Their love didn't fade when they left this world: it became a guiding warmth, reminding you of their laughter, dreams, and joy. Being bruised but beautiful means embracing the pain, allowing it to shape you, and carrying that love as proof that something so pure and eternal can never truly be lost.

"Even through tears, you are radiant."

You are radiant because your light comes from a place deeper than pain. It comes from love, resilience, and the courage to keep moving forward.
It's ok to cry, it's ok to fall apart. But never forget that your strength lies in your vulnerability, and that makes you beautiful.
Tears don't diminish your beauty; they reflect the strength it takes to feel, to grieve, and to   heal.

"Healing is not forgetting, it's learning to carry the love forward."

Grief doesn't mean you leave the memories behind. You carry them with you, letting them shape your future in meaningful ways.

"Bruises fade, but beauty grows in their place."

Bruises fade; leaving behind more than just healed skin- they leave wisdom, strength, and a deeper understanding of life's fragility and resilience. Each bruise tells a story of pain endured and lessons learned. But as they fade, beauty grows in their place. This beauty isn't superficial: it's the quiet confidence of a soul that has faced hardship and refused to be defined by it. It's the compassion that blossoms from knowing struggle and the grace that comes from rising above it. Bruises may mark the body for a time, but the beauty they leave behind is eternal.

"You are allowed to grieve and grow at the same time."

There's no timeline for healing. Take each step forward at your own pace, knowing that sadness and joy, grief and growth can coexist at the same time, each shaping you in different ways. While your heart aches for what was lost, it also learns to hold onto love, hope, and strength. Growth doesn't mean forgetting; it means honoring your pain while moving forward with the lessons it has taught you.

"The most beautiful flowers grow from the deepest wounds in the earth."

From wounds beauty blooms and life is renewed.
Where the soil has been pressed, broken, and enriched by time. From those depths, life finds its way, pushing through darkness to reach the light. In the same way, our most profound growth comes from the wounds and struggles that shape us.

"Though we are bruised, we are never defeated, for the beauty lies in the healing of our souls."

The beauty lies not in the absence of pain but in the healing of our souls- the way we rise, mend, and grow from what tried to break us.

Every mark tells a story of survival and strength. It is in this healing that our true resilience and radiance are revealed.

"Healing begins when you stop hiding your scars and start embracing your story."

Scars aren't meant to be hidden; they are proof of battles fought and survived. When you share your story, you allow others to see the beauty in your strength and inspire them to embrace their own journey of healing.

"Beauty is not the absence of scars but the stories they tell of survival and love."

Your scars are a testament to the love you've carried. They remind us that even in the face of hardship, love and resilience can triumph, leaving behind a beauty that is deeper and more profound than perfection.

"You were bruised but never stopped being beautiful, for beauty is in the heart that loves through the pain."

Love transforms pain into an everlasting beauty.
Even in the depths of sorrow, your beauty never faded. It wasn't in perfection, but in the love that endured the kindness that remained, and the strength that carried you forward. Every tear, every scar, every moment of resilience only deepened the radiance within you. For beauty is not in what is unbroken, it is in the heart that chooses to love, even through the pain.

"The beauty of life isn't in avoiding the pain but in discovering the strength to keep going."

Strength shines brightest through the storms we endure. The beauty of life isn't found in a path without pain, but in the strength we uncover along the way. Every trial, every tear, every moment of heartache shapes us, revealing a resilience we never knew we had. It's in the rising after the fall, the hope after the hurt, and the courage to keep moving forward. True beauty isn't a life without struggle, but in a spirit that refuses to be defeated.

"Though my heart is bruised, it's still full of beauty- every beat carrying their laughter, dreams, and light."

Even though my heart is bruised, it remains a vessel of beauty, a reflection of the love we shared. Each beat carries their laughter, their dreams, and the light they brought into my life. The pain reminds me of how deeply I loved and how deeply I was loved in return. Even in sorrow, their essence lives within me, filling the cracks and warmth and hope. My heart may be bruised, but it beats with strength only love can give.

"Grief breaks us, grace mends us, and growth transforms us into more than we ever thought we could be."

Grief, Grace, and Growth
Grief shakes us, leaving us broken in ways we never imagined. But grace steps in, mending the shattered pieces with love and strength. Through that grace, we grow-reshaped, refined, and transformed into more than we ever thought we could be. What once felt like an ending becomes the beginning of something deeper, a journey of resilience, wisdom, and renewed purpose.

"Beauty rises from the ashes of pain; through every storm, his love remains."

Out of every hardship,
 God brings renewal. What
  was once broken is restored,
 and what was lost is made new.
  His love is the constant that
 carries us, turning sorrow into
 strength and pain into purpose.

"Every Fall taught me to Stand Taller"

With each stumble, I found strength, with each setback, I gained wisdom. What once knocked me down now lifts me higher, shaping me into someone stronger than before.

"The storm may have cracked my shell, but it revealed my strength within."

Pain has a way of peeling back the surface, exposing parts of us we never knew existed. What was once hidden by fear or doubt becomes clear through struggle. The storm didn't break you — it introduced you to the warrior you've always been. Every scar is proof that you fought to stay standing, even when the winds were strongest.

"Bruised but beautiful, scarred yet whole, God's love is the anchor of my soul."

Life may leave its marks, but they do not define me - God's love does. In every trial, He holds me steady, turning pain into strength and scars into reminders of his unshakable grace.

"Life's trials may bruise us, but they also reveal our inner beauty."

Hardships may leave marks on the outside, but they bring forth the quiet strength, compassion, and grace within. It's in our broken moments that the true beauty of who we are begins to shine.

"Consider it pure joy, whenever you face trials of many kinds."

Adversity acts as a sculptor, chipping away our outer layers to unveil the resilience and grace within. Each challenge we face highlights the strength and beauty of our spirit, demonstrating that true beauty emerges not in the absence of hardship, but through our courageous response to it.

"Every bruise is a brushstroke in God's masterpiece of our lives."

For we are God's handiwork, created in Christ to do good works. Each challenge we face adds depth and color to the canvas of our existence, contributing to the unique masterpiece that God is crafting within us.

"In the face of trials, we discover the depth of our courage and grace."

When challenges arise, they serve as mirrors reflecting our inner strength. Each obstacle becomes an opportunity to delve deeper into our reservoir of resilience, revealing the facets of courage we may not have known existed.

"Rising from the ashes, I found my wings, wings forged by trials, lifted by faith."

What once felt like the end, became the beginning of my transformation. The fire that tried to consume me instead refined me, and from the ashes, I found my wings. With every lesson, every tear, and every moment of faith, I grew stronger. I was not defeated, I was remade, ready to rise higher than before.

"I may stumble on the path, but I will not stop walking – grace steadies every step."

Every journey has uneven ground, moments when doubt or fear makes us falter. But even in the stumble, we are not alone. God's grace catches us, lifts us, and gently guides us forward. What once felt like a setback becomes part of the strength that carries us ahead.

"In the midst of our struggles, God's light makes us shine beautifully."

Even our darkest moments, God's light never far from us. Our trials may cast shadows, but his presence turns them into a glow of resilience and faith. Like a diamond formed under pressure, we emerge from our struggles reflecting his love, grace, and strength for the world to see.

"In our weakest moments, God's strength makes us beautiful."

When we feel broken and weary, God's strength lifts us. He turns our frailty into grace, our sorrow into purpose, and our pain into a testimony of his power. In him, our weakness becomes a radiant beauty that shines from within.

"Our scars tell a story of survival and God's unwavering grace."

Each scar is a reminder that we have overcome what once tried to break us. They are not marks of defeat but of resilience, proof that God's grace carried us through. What once brought pain, now tells a story of his healing, his faithfulness, and his power to restore.

"Though your arms may feel empty, your heart overflows with the love you shared. That love will never fade."

Love is not bound by physical presence. The love you shared is eternal, living on in every cherished memory, every whispered prayer, and every moment of quiet reflection. It is a love that fills the heart, even when the world feels hollow- a love that will never fade, because it was born of a bond that nothing, not even loss, can break. Let love be your strength and your guide.

"The scars you carry aren't signs of defeat — they're proof you survived the flames and rose stronger than the fire."

Life's trials may leave scars, but those scars tell a story of survival. The flames that threatened to destroy you now illuminate your path, reminding you of your strength and resilience with every step forward.

"Pain shapes us but love rebuilds us"

The weight of pain may feel unbearable, but love gives us the tools to rebuild what was broken. In love, we find the courage to piece ourselves back together, creating something even more beautiful than before.

"True beauty is found in courage to rise again"

Each time you rise after falling, you add to the masterpiece of your life. Bruises may mark your journey, but they are reminders that you never gave up, and that resilience is the truest form of beauty.

"She gathered the pieces of her brokenness and built something unshakable."

Healing is not about returning to who you were—it's about becoming someone even more powerful. When life shatters what was, you are given the sacred chance to rebuild with purpose. What you create from your pain becomes your legacy: resilient, rooted, and radiant. Beauty doesn't hide in perfection—it shines brightest in redemption.

"Even in the storm, there is beauty in the way you hold on."

Life's storms may rage around you, but your steady grip on hope and love is a quiet act of defiance. That perseverance, even in the face of chaos, reveals the beauty of a soul that refuses to give up.

"Grace is finding beauty in the ashes of what you thought would destroy you."

When the dust settles, what remains isn't just the remnants of what was lost- it's the foundation for what is yet to come. In the ashes, grace allows beauty to rise, more radiant than before.

"Grief is love with no place to go. Let that love be your strength as you honor your child's memory."

Grief lingers because love remains. Though your arms may be empty, your heart still holds the warmth of their presence. Let that love guide you, not as a weight of sorrow, but as a light that honors their memory with every step you take.

"I didn't ask for the storm, but I learned how to dance in the rain."

Life threw me into grief's downpour, yet in the puddles of sorrow, I found rhythm, grace, and a strength I never knew I carried.

"The cracks in my heart let the light of love shine through."

Brokenness did not make me less; it made me luminous. My pain became a window where love beamed brighter than ever.

"Bruised souls carry the gentlest love."

Having known suffering, I now love with tender hands. Compassion was birthed from pain, and kindness became her crown.

"Out of the ashes of loss, I rose with a heart full of fire."

The world tried to break me, but the heat of grief refined me. Now I walk boldly, flawed, fierce, and glowing.

"Beauty bloomed in the very place my heart broke."

I returned to the memory that crushed me –
and in that sacred soil, a garden of strength
and softness took root.

"I carry grief like a rose- thorny, beautiful, and real."

Pain never left my hands empty; it gave me pedals and thorns. Both reminded me I was still alive, still loving.

"Even her silence was sacred, wrapped in the whispers of sorrow and strength."

When she had no words left, her presence spoke volumes. Grief made her quiet, but it didn't take her voice.

"My smile didn't mean I wasn't hurting, it meant I was healing."

Joy returned, not as loud laughter, but a soft reminder that I could still feel, still hope, still live.

"Pain taught me how to pray with my whole being."

I knelt not just with words, but with tears, with silence, with aching. My prayers became lifelines through the storms.

"I didn't just survive, I softened and still chose love.

Surviving is one thing. But to still love, to still trust, to still give – that's where my true beauty rose.

"My scars are not shame - they are sacred reminders that I   lived through the unthinkable   and kept going."

Each mark is a story, a breath I didn't know I had the strength to take. They whisper of courage born in the storm.

"She wore grief like lace, fragile yet intricate, painful, yet beautiful."

In her mourning, there was elegance. In her sorrow, depth. And in it all, she remained softly strong.

"She's not healing to forget, she's healing to honor."

Every step forward carries the memory with grace. Love doesn't leave- it simply learns to walk with her.

"Her beauty didn't bloom in ease- it was born in endurance."

Through every ache, she built resilience. Not overnight, but day by day, in silence, in tears, in hope.

"The heart break didn't end her –It deepened her."

Like rain that carves valleys, loss reshaped her spirit and in that safety hollow, new beauty took root.

"She doesn't just survive she carries light for others, still walking through the dark"

Her pain became a lantern. Her words, a shelter. She *is* the guide she once needed.

"She let the broken pieces shine. And that's when she realized- they made mosaic."

What once felt shattered now glows with meaning. Beauty, not in spite of the cracks, but because of them.

"Grief didn't make her less, it made her tender, more fierce, more real.

It stripped away the surface and revealed her soul - vulnerable and vast, soft and unshakable.

"Even with empty arms, she holds a love so full, it fills every room she walks into."

Her loss didn't take love, it magnified it, echoing through her every word, gesture, and breath.

"She doesn't seek to be the same - she seeks to be whole in a new way."

Healing didn't mean going back. It meant becoming, transforming, and blooming forward with love in every step.

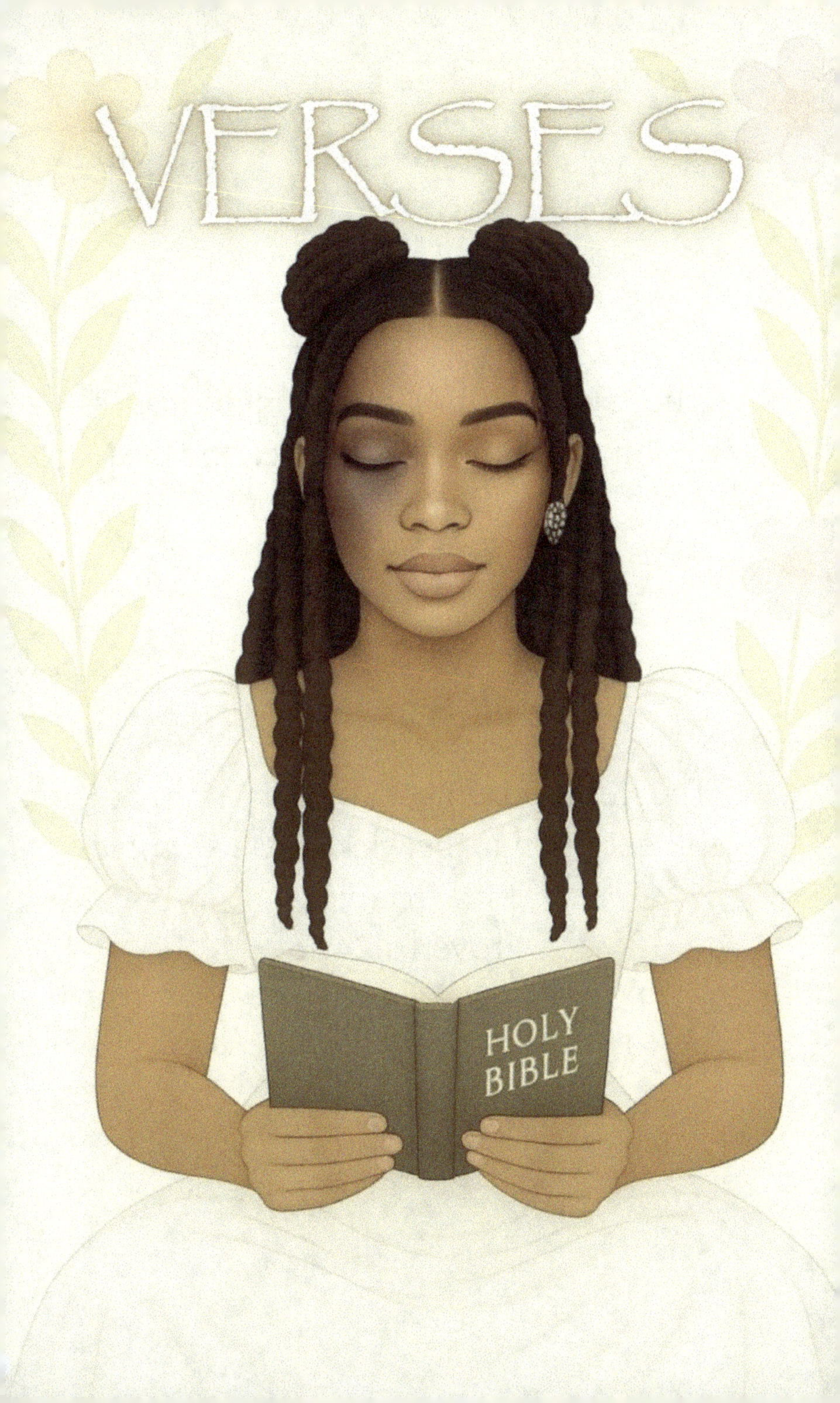
VERSES
HOLY BIBLE

"Those who lead many to righteousness
will shine like the stars forever and ever."
Daniel 12:3

"The righteous may fall seven times but
still get up, but the wicked will stumble
into trouble."
Proverbs 24:16

"And now these three remain: faith, hope and love. But the greatest of these is love."
1 Corinthians 13:13

"Though he may stumble, he will not fall, for the lord upholds him with his hand."
Psalms 37:24

"Though I have fallen, I will rise. Though I sit in darkness, the lord will be my light."
Micah 7:8

"I will lift up my eyes to the hills, from whence comes my help. My help comes from the lord, who made heaven and earth."
Psalms 121:1-2

"We are hard pressed on every side, but not crushed struck down, but not destroyed."
2 Corinthians 4:8-9

"The lord is my rock, my fortress, and my deliverer."
Psalms 18:2

"He comforts us so that we can comfort those in any trouble."
2 Corinthians 1:4

"The Lord is close to the brokenhearted and saves those who are crushed in spirit."
Psalms 34:18

"Those who sow with tears will reap with songs of joy."
Psalms 126:5

"My grace is sufficient for you, for my power is made perfect in weakness."
2 Corinthians 12:9

"And we know that in all things God works for the good of those who love him."
Romans 8:28

"Because of the lord's great love we are not consumed, for his compassions never fail. They are new every morning."
Lamentation 3:22-23

"But he knows the way that I take: when he has tested me, I will come forth as gold."
Job 23:10

"Behold, I am making all things new."
Revelation 21:5

"See, I am doing a new thing. I am making a way in the wilderness."
Isaiah 43:19

"Blessed are those who mourn, for they shall be comforted."
Matthew 5:4

"To bestow on them a crown of beauty instead of ashes."
Isaiah 61:3

"When I said, my foot is slipping, your unfailing love, Lord, supported me. When anxiety was great within me, your consolation brought me joy."
Psalm 94:18-19

"He has made everything beautiful in its time."
Ecclesiastes 3:11

"Peace I leave with you; my peace I give to you. Not as the world giveth, give I unto you. Let not your heart be troubled, neither let it be afraid."
John 14:27

"In the day when I cried out, you answered me, and made me bold with strength in my soul."
Psalms 138:3

"Cast your burdens on the lord, and he shall sustain you; he shall never permit the righteous to be removed."
Psalms 55:22

"In this world you will have trouble. But take heart! I have overcome the world."
John 16:33

"But we have this treasure in jars of clay to show that this all –surpassing power is from God and not from us.
2 Corinthians 4:7

"I consider that our present sufferings are not worth comparing with the glory that will be revealed in us.
Romans 8:18

"But those who hope in the lord will renew their strength. They will soar on wings like eagles."
Isaiah 40:31

"Weeping may endure for a night, but joy comes in the morning light."
Psalms 30:5

"He will wipe every tear from their eyes. There will be no more death or mourning or crying or pain.
Revelation 21:4

STRENGTH FORGED IN STORMS

Though storms have raged and left their mark, I carry light within the dark. Each scar, a story, each tear a song, yet love and strength have made me strong.

A MELODY THAT NEVER FADES

Your child's love, a song so sweet, a melody
that time can't beat.
Though silence falls where
laughter played, their love
remains – it will not fade.

WHISPERS OF FOREVER

Through tearful nights and empty days, their
light still finds the quiet ways.
A whisper soft, a memory near, they're in your
heart forever here.

RISING WITH GRACE

I may have stumbled, I may have cried, but
God beside me, I rise with pride.

BEAUTY BORN FROM BRUISES

I'm bruised but not broken, bent but
not lost, through trials and fire,
I've paid the cost. Yet beauty
blooms where pain once grew' a
testament to all I've been through.
I rise, I shine I stand tall –
Bruised but beautiful, through it all.

STRENGTH IN THE BRUISES

"Bruised but not broken, weary but still strong,
God's love has kept me all along."

HELD BY GRACE

"Every wound I carry tells a story of grace –
God's hands have held me in every place."

A LOVE THAT NEVER LEAVES

"The days are long, the nights are wide, but they are there, right by your side. A bond like this, will never part - their home is always in your heart."

SOFT LIKE FAITH

"She didn't need armor, didn't need fire,
My softness became what lifted her higher.
Grace was her banner, faith was her thread,
She bloomed from the tears her soul quietly
shed."

UNBREAKABLE BOND

"The bond you shared can never break,
No storm of grief it's strength can take.
Though loss may ache and time feels slow, their
love within will always grow."

WHISPERED COMFORT

"When shadows fall and hope feels small, their
spirit answers every call.
In every smile, in every breeze,
their love still sets your heart at ease."

ETERNAL LOVE, HEALING WOUNDS

"The pain you feel, so deep so real, is love's
reminder: wounds can heal.
Their joy is now the stars above, a timeless gift,
eternal love."

FOREVER BY YOUR SIDE

"The days are long the nights are wide, but
they are there, right by your side.
A bond like this will never part-their home is
always in your heart."

GUIDING LIGHT

"Their memory glows, a guiding light, to lead you through the darkest night. With every step, their love you'll find, a gentle voice within your mind."

LOVE'S UNBROKEN MELODY

"Grief is heavy, love is strong, a rhythm in
your heart's own song.
Each moment lived, they're living too, forever
bound by love to you."

WAVES OF THEIR LOVE

"Though hands can't touch and eyes can't see, their spirit moves like waves at sea. Through every tide, through highs and lows, their love within you always flows."

ENDLESS ECHOES

"Their journey's pause is not the end, for love like this will never bend. They live in dreams, in skies of blue- Their love is endless, just like you."

SHE IS THE PROOF

"She is the proof that broken can shine, that
hearts stitched with tears still beat in time.
Bruised but beautiful, tried and true-
She is what healing chooses to do."

NOT THE END

"It wasn't the end when the world caved in
It was the start of where strength begins.

Though loss shook me, it could not erase
The radiant light from my soul embrace."

IN THE SHAPE OF HER

"There's beauty in the way she moves,
Carrying sorrow that time can't smooth.
Yet in every step, grace can be seen-
A woman made of love and in between."

WHEN SILENCE SPEAKS

"She stopped explaining her sorrow one day,
And let her silence quietly pray.
Stillness became her sacred ground-
And in that hush, her healing was found."

SHE WEEPS, SHE RISES

"Let her cry. Let her break. Let her fall to her knees.
From the ashes, she gathers the piece she needs.
Not all warriors roar, not all angels have wings-
Some women wear bruises like royalty's rings."

CRACKED BUT CALLED

"I thought I was broken, too flawed to be
whole,
But God used the cracks to pour light through
my soul.
My scars were the maps that pointed to grace,
A beauty that time nor pain could erase."

HEAVEN IN HER HEART

"A whisper, a memory, a name in the wind,
She lost her child, but love didn't end.
Heaven lives now in each word and each smile,
Though bruised, she walks forward every mile."

PETALS FROM PAIN

"She cried in the dark, alone with the ache,
Yet morning brought beauty that no one could
fake.
Her grief held the seeds of something brand
new,
A garden of strength where hope gently grew."

CRACKS OF GOLD

"I am not broken, only cracked,
Where light seeps in and won't turn back.
My wounds may sting, my soul may cry,
But beauty lives where pain did lie."

GRACE IN HER GRAZE

She weeps in silence, walks with grace,
With every tear, she finds her place.
A gentle power, a quiet might,
Bruised but glowing, full of light.

FROM ASHES, A BLOOM

The fire raged, but didn't kill-
It forged a heart with deeper will.
Ashes settled, petals grew,
From loss, a garden born anew.

STILL I RISE, SOFTLY

"Not in thunder, not in pride,
But with tears I've not denied.
My strength is wrapped in gentle things-
Like whispered prayers and angel wings."

A SCARRED SYMPHONY

"Every scar a note I sing,
Each one adds a sacred ring.
I'm not a song of pain alone,
But of healing, etched in bone."

GENTLE WARRIOR

"She fought without raising her voice,
Her strength was in every quiet choice.
To keep on loving, to still believe
Even as her soul would grieve."

WINGS FROM WOUNDS

"The pain once pinned me to the floor,
Now I have wings I never wore.
Not despite the ache, but through it, true-
I found the skies I never knew."

TEARS LIKE RAIN

"Tears may fall like heavy rain,
But flowers bloom from storms and pain.
So let me weep, and let me grow-
My soul knows what the roots don't show."

THE BEAUTY SHE CARRIED

"It wasn't in her hair or dress,
But in the way she bore distress.
A lovely heart, a soul set free-
Her beauty lived in memory."

CROWN OF QUIET STRENGTH

"She never asked to wear this crown,
Yet wears it even kneeling down.
With grief she walks, but walks in grace-
A bruised queen with a glowing face."

THE BLOOM WITHIN

"Though outward joy had once grown dim,
Inside of her bloomed a quiet hymn.
She sang of love and pain and peace-
A beauty that will never cease."

STITCHED BY GRACE

"Torn by sorrow, frayed by time,
But stitched by grace in every line.
Not flawless now, but richly sewn,
Each seam a story she has known."

LOVES IMPRINT

"Your voice is gone; your touch has flown,
But love still whispers through my bones.
You shaped the way I break and bend.
The love that bruised me is my friend."

CARRYING YOU

"I carry you in breath and prayer,
In sunsets soft and morning air.
You're gone but beauty still remains
In all my joy and all my pains."

THE TENDER KIND

"Her strength was not the sharp, loud kind-
It flowed through every tear she'd find.
Soft yet strong, still standing tall
Beauty wrapped in rise and fall."

MADE OF MORE

"She thought she broke- but found instead,
A woman new, where old grief bled.
More than pain, she is the proof-
That storms can't steal a living truth."

GARDEN OF GRIEF

"Her tears watered what once was bare,
Grief became a garden there.
From loss and longing, faith had grown
And beauty bloomed from seeds unknown."

HOLLOW AND HOLY

"The hollow in her heart remains,
Yet somehow sings through all the pains.
She's sacred now in ways unplanned-
Held gently in God's quiet hand."

THE BEAUTY AFTER

"There's beauty in the after part,
The tender ache, the softer heart.
When all has fallen, she still stands-
With open soul and open hands."

BRUISED BUT BEAUTIFUL

"She is the moon with shadowed face,
Yet still commands the stars and space.
Her bruises do not dim her light-
They shimmer softly through the night."

LET US PRAY

Dear God, mend the broken pieces of my heart. I bring you the weight of my grief and ask for the *balm* of your peace. Teach me how to breathe through sorrow and trust you in the silence.

Amen.

PRAYERS FOR STRENGTH IN WEAKNESS

Lord, I am weary. Be my strength when I can no longer walk alone. Let your presence lift my soul and remind me that I am never truly alone.

Amen.

PRAYER TO FEEL GOD'S NEARNESS

God of all comfort, wrap your arms around me today. Let me feel your nearness in every moment, even when the pain makes you feel far away.

Amen.

PRAYER FOR DAILY RENEWAL

Father, renew my spirit today. Wash over me with fresh hope and awaken the joy that sorrow tried to bury. I received your peace.

Amen

PRAYER FOR COURAGE AFTER LOSS

Lord, help me to face each new day with courage. I may be wounded, but I walk forward knowing that you walk with me.

Amen.

PRAYER FOR BEAUTY AFTER THE STORM

Heavenly father, show me the beauty rising from my ashes. Let me see glimpses of new beginnings, even in the aftermath of loss.

Amen.

PRAYER FOR LETTING GO

God, I release what I can't change. Help me trust that you are holding what I can't carry. Let peace flow into the space where pain once ruled.

Amen.

PRAYER FOR A WEARY HEART

Lord, my heart is tired. Fill me with quiet strength. Let your rest be my refuge, and your love my lifeline.

Amen.

PRAYER FOR GRACE TO HEAL SLOWLY

Father, I give myself to heal slowly. You are patient with me, so I will be patient with myself. Carry me through each step of this healing journey.

Amen.

PRAYER FOR THE BROKEN AND BELOVED

Dear God, remind me that even broken, I am beloved. Even bruised, I am Beautiful. Even grieving, I am still yours.

Amen.

PRAYER FOR THE JOURNEY AHEAD

God, the road before me feels long and unknown. But I trust that you walk before me. Light my path with hope.

Amen.

PRAYER FOR QUIET COMFORT

Lord, meet me in the quiet places.
Where words fail and tears fall,
speak peace into my soul and hold
me until I remember joy again.

Amen.

PRAYER FOR RESTORATION

Father, restore the places in me that feel lost. Breathe life into the parts of my heart that forgot how to feel. Rebuild me gently.

Amen.

PRAYER FOR TRUST AFTER LOSS

God, it's hard to trust again after heartbreak. Teach me to open my hands, to believe that love still lives, and that you still have more for me.

Amen.

PRAYER FOR PEACE IN THE MIDDLE

Dear Lord, I'm not at the beginning, and I haven't reached the end- but I need peace right here in the middle. Be my calm. Be my center.

Amen.

PRAYER OF THANKS FOR TODAY

Even in sorrow, thank you for breath in my lungs. Thank you for another sunrise. Thank you for staying with me while I heal.

Amen.

PRAYER FOR HOPE RISING

Lord, let hope rise again. Let it be stronger than fear, louder than doubt, and more faithful than my circumstances.

Amen.

PRAYER FOR A NEW HEARTBEAT

God, give my heart a new rhythm. Let it beat with courage, love, and expectation for what's ahead -not just sorrow for what's behind.

Amen.

PRAYER FOR STILLNESS

Lord, I give you my chaos. Quiet my soul so I can hear you again. Remind me that I don't need all the answers to be held by you.

Amen.

PRAYER FOR THE MORNING AFTER THE STORM

Thank you, God, that even after the storm, the sun still rises. I am still here. And you are still good.

Amen.

MEDITATIONS

MEDITATIONS FOR HEALING AND RENEWAL

Sit quietly and breathe in the word "peace". Exhale the word "release". With each breath, let your heart rest in the truth that God is still near, even in this moment of pain.

MEDITATE

Picture yourself walking beside still waters.
You are not alone. The Shepherd is near,
guiding you gently toward healing and calm.

MEDITATE

Place your hand over your heart. Whisper: "This heart has endured much, but it is still beating with purpose. I am still here. I am still loved".

MEDITATE

Close your eyes and imagine your tears being caught by Gods hand. None are wasted. Each one waters the soil of something new about to grow.

MEDITATE

As you inhale, repeat: "God is with me." As you exhale, whisper: "I am safe to heal." Do this slowly and intentionally, letting your spirit soften.

MEDITATE

Picture the scars on your heart as golden lines, like Kintsugi pottery. They do not make you less- they tell your story with beauty and grace.

MEDITATE

Visualize the morning sun touching your face. With every ray, a new part of you awakens: joy, courage, gentleness. You are becoming whole again.

MEDITATE

Hold your grief like a fragile flower. Let it be what it is- precious, painful, part of your journey. And know that even this has purpose.

MEDITATE

Imagine a warm light pouring into your chest.
It pushes out fear, sorrow, and shame.
What's left is stillness. What's left is you –
healing.

MEDITATE

Let your mind rest on the truth: You don't have to be perfect to be beautiful. Even bruised, you shine. Let that be enough today.

MEDITATE

Breathe in deeply and imagine light entering your body with every inhale. Picture each breath filling the dark places with warmth and healing.

MEDITATE

Whisper: "I give myself grace." Let your shoulders fall. Release the pressure to be okay. Just be present, that is enough.

MEDITATE

Sit with your grief like an old friend. It has shaped you, but it does not define you. With every passing moment, healing is unfolding.

MEDITATE

Imagine your soul as a garden. Today, you're planting seeds: rest, faith, forgiveness. Water them with stillness. Let them grow.

MEDITATE

Think of the love that remains – love that no loss can erase. Let it wrap around you like a soft blanket. Let it remind you that love never dies.

MEDITATE

With each breathe, say: "I let go of shame. I welcome healing." Let your body soften. Let your spirit open. Let your healing begin.

MEDITATE

Feel your heartbeat and know-it's a rhythm of resilience. It has carried you through storms. It will carry you into peace.

MEDITATE

Envision yourself placing your pain in God's
hand. It's safe there.
You don't have to hold it alone anymore.

MEDITATE

Visualize a gentle wind blowing through your soul, sweeping away the debris of grief, and leaving behind only what is sacred and soft.

Today, rest in this truth:
Even broken things can become blessings.
Even your story will bloom in beauty
again.

- AUTHOR TRUDY M. JOHNSON

MY BEAUTIFUL THOUGHTS

"Even here, even now – I am still becoming."

BRUISED BUT STILL I WRITE

"I am healing, even when it doesn't feel like it."

WHISPERS FROM MY HEART

_____

_____

_____

_____

_____

_____

_____

_____

_____

_____

_____

_____

"Your words matter – even the broken, scattered ones."

LIGHT AFTER LOSS

"Today I will honor my heart by listening to it."

SACRED SPACE TO BREATHE

"May this space carry the truth of your becoming."

QUIET STRENGTH

_____

_____

_____

_____

_____

_____

_____

_____

_____

_____

_____

_____

"Your story is not over, keep writing"